Other Books by Kate Vredevoogd

From the Same Quiver: A Confessional Tale of Wanderlust, Friendship and the Pursuit of Self-Identity

Words of Wellbeing, A to Z

Palabras de Bienestar (Spanish Edition)

"This is an important book on living, and dying. Kate is a beautiful writer and has captured the eleven days of her father's journey out of this life as seen and felt through his daughter's eyes and heart. As a family friend I am so grateful that I was personally able to witness the incredible love, sorrow and peace of Bruce's journey. A book you will not soon forget."

—Julia Bozzo, Executive Director at NorthWest Therapeutic Riding Center

"This is an inspiring and rare gem of a book! You will feel and experience Kate's honesty and tenderness in this loving tribute to her dear dad. In her transformative healing journey through illness, dying, death, and grief she shares her insights and wisdom gained along the way. I am truly touched by and appreciate her authenticity and dedication to healing her heart and soul. The big message is that healing is possible and what matters most, and what we carry forward, is Love."

—Andrea Fenwick, Death Doula, Social Worker, and Hospice Volunteer

"As a death doula and someone who supports people in the process of grief, I believe that Kate really captures the essence of what is possible for families when they choose to witness death as a sacred experience. She shows us that death can facilitate a deeper healing than we know is possible and create a closeness between family members. She shows us the bravery it takes to stand by her father during the time that he chose VSED, and the intimate details of his life that will be sure to bring tears to your eyes. This book would be an enormous support to those who are professionals working with the dying, for those who are dying and the loved ones supporting them. I read this book in one sitting! Very well written, heartwarming and captivating. May you receive the wisdom and medicine from the intimacy of Kate, and her father's death story."

—Micaela Musterer, Death doula, Grief practitioner, Community Organizer

"Kate shares a testimony few have experienced. I took a journey that paralleled hers with my mother and dementia, and I have encountered death by my profession for the past thirty-five years, but this story of Kate's experience of her father's chosen path took me to a much deeper level, spiritually. A very enlightening and powerful story, which reflects on life's greater meaning."

—Melissa Bradshaw, LPN

WITH INTENTION
A VSED Story

Kate Vredevoogd

With Intention (A VSED Story)
Copyright © 2023 by Kate Vredevoogd, Wanderlust Words Publications

For more about this author please visit www.wanderlustwords.com

This author is not engaged in rendering medical or psychological services, and this book is not intended as a guide to diagnose or treat medical or psychological problems. If you require medical, psychological, or other expert assistance, please seek the services of your own physician or mental health professional.

All rights reserved. No part of this publication may be reproduced, distributed, or transmitted in any form or by any means, including photocopying, recording, or other electronic or mechanical methods, without the prior written permission of the publisher, except in the case of brief quotations embodied in critical reviews and certain other noncommercial uses permitted by copyright law. Please do not participate in or encourage piracy of copyrighted materials in violation of the author's rights.

Editing by The Pro Book Editor
Interior and Cover Design by IAPS.rocks
Cover art by Miette Bennich IG @miettepaints

eBook ISBN: 978-1-7341839-2-4
paperback ISBN: 978-1-7341839-3-1

    Main category—SELF-HELP / Death, Grief, Bereavement
    Other category—FAMILY & RELATIONSHIPS / Death, Grief, Bereavement

First Edition

For Tony. May you rest peacefully.

For Mom. Thank you. *Thank you.* I love you.

Prologue

He's dreaming. Or maybe he's moving his lips because his mouth is dry. His last drink of water was yesterday evening. All I can do for him now is spritz some water in his mouth to alleviate the dryness. He looks so small and frail in the hospital bed that was put in his bedroom, but his presence remains powerful.

Everything he does is with intention. Even this. Even death.

My dad doesn't need size or volume to make an echo—his power has a great gentleness to it. The softer he speaks, the more closely people listen. Even when the Parkinson's Disease weakens his voice to a whisper, sometimes leaving just the intention of the words resting on his lips, we still hang on to every one. He's always been insightful, but the more his communication is limited, the more profound he becomes.

It took me getting space to appreciate my dad's wisdom, but now I can't imagine my life without it. The way he waits, taking everything in, observing the back and forth of the discussion, and then, at the exact right moment of pause, offers his succinct distillation, so simple and obvious that you know you've just heard the truth. His advice is clear, cuts right through the bullshit, and is given sparingly enough to be considered a gift of tremendous value. "What would Bruce do?" has become a family catchphrase.

To complement his moments of Zen wisdom, he also knows when humor is the right medicine. His accuracy is flawless when finding the sweet spot between irreverence and grace. And to compliment his accuracy, I remember him keeping a tiny squirt gun in the door of his Ford Ranger while I was growing up. In the summers when we all drove with the windows down, he'd scan the cars next to us for serious faces and practice that accuracy. After getting hit with the tiny stream of water and seeing a goofy dad with a plastic squirt gun and his five-year-old daughter next to him, no one could keep their own inner child from bursting into laughter. He is the archetypal trickster. To him, life is serious, but never too serious for the right joke.

Over the years, I've seen him coax countless people, including grocery store cashiers, out of their bad moods. With a little tact and just enough teasing, he'd get them to crack a smile, and even laugh at themselves, turning what could have been a contagion of negativity into a nourishing and lighthearted exchange.

Chapter 1
June 2014

My dad's journey with Parkinson's officially began the day of my wedding, seven years ago, when I was twenty-four. It was a beautiful celebration on their farmhouse in the countryside where I grew up, just outside of Bellingham, Washington. My dad built that house when I was a kid, with the help of a team and his best friend, Tony. Dad put love and passion into every project he took on. The interior was designed with the artistry of a master woodworker, which he was. It had high ceilings and large windows that looked out over acres of pasture, where the horses would gallop and the occasional cow would graze. My bedroom was on the side of the house that faced the forest, and the year my dad decided to install owl boxes, I became very familiar with the sound of screeching teenage owls.

The farm had never looked better than on that torrid summer's day in June of 2014, when I declared my love to my new Spanish husband. There were more flowers than I had ever seen in one place. Poppies in vases, wildflowers hanging from the apple trees, flowers of all colors, shapes, and sizes on every surface. The garden was resplendent. My dad's friends played funky jazz music that we all danced barefoot to. Although that marriage wasn't everlasting, the wedding was a day of great joy that I'll never forget or regret.

As the evening progressed, my dad took an occasional swig from the whiskey bottle, as a good cowboy would. I had never seen him overly drunk before, so I didn't know if that's what this was, but I noticed something different about him. The way he had lost some control of his body didn't seem exactly like the slurred stumbling of intoxication. I didn't spend much time thinking about it, but it was almost as if there was something else at play. Years later, my mom told me that it was that night when she truly knew something was wrong. When she put him to bed and he passed out, stinking of whiskey, she noticed his left arm moving on its own. It was the Parkinson's tremor confirming her suspicions.

After that, she came back out and refilled her gin and tonic, laughed with my friends, and had a blast by the campfire until four in the morning. There I was, twenty-four years old and drunk on love and Kentucky bourbon, excited to go back to Spain and start a new life. Meanwhile, my mom was secretly processing the enormous implications of my dad's tiny tremor, her mind and heart filling with dread.

They didn't tell me my dad was sick until after the wedding, after I had returned to Spain. I get it—they wanted me to have the wedding I deserved and didn't want my decisions regarding the direction I steered my life to be swayed off course by any dark and stormy winds. But I have to ask myself, would I have done things differently had I known sooner? Would I have stopped the cart before it parked permanently on the other side of the world? Considering the long phase of denial that ensued, which I was arguably still in, even then as he literally lay on his deathbed, it's hard to say.

Chapter 2
January 2020

Degenerative diseases are like black mold. You notice a few spots here, a few patches there. You scrub it off with some harsh chemicals, but the spores linger. And then, after a few years of downplaying the gravity of the problem that these little signs are pointing to, and spot treating the symptoms because it's all you know how to do, you move a piece of furniture and find that it was covering a massive infestation. And then, one bad winter hits, which for my dad was the winter of 2020, and the whole house is taken out by the mold.

One of his first major symptoms was something he referred to as "brain fog." It was a sort of blurriness and heaviness that settled in over his mind like a thick blanket of evening fog covering the hayfield. It snuck in without warning and left him powerless. He couldn't react, or process, or even think. It would happen at home, and he'd have to excuse himself for a few hours until the fog lifted. It would happen at dinner parties with friends. It would happen at the grocery store.

The brain fog was often accompanied by a sudden and dramatic fatigue. The wave would wash over him, and he'd be swept away despite his efforts to stay awake and on solid ground. When this happened to him at the grocery store, he'd have to abandon his full shopping cart and go out to the car to take a nap. If his cart was there twenty minutes later, he could continue his shopping. If not, he'd have to turn around and go home empty-handed. I can't imagine the frustration and feelings of helplessness it must have caused him.

The first few times I went home to visit after the diagnosis, his Parkinson's Disease was easy for me to ignore. His battle was mostly internal until the final few years, and he spent more time on his inner battlefield than any of us on the outside were aware of. He'd occasionally get up in the middle of a conversation and close himself in his room, but for me it was an "out of sight, out of mind" situation. It's not like I didn't *want* to know what he was going through, but I was holding on with a white-knuckled grip to the story I desperately needed to believe that my dad wasn't really that ill. If I had truly put myself in his shoes, I'd have had to let go of that story and accept that he was slowly being swept out to sea.

In January of 2020, we took a family vacation to the small coastal town on the Pacific coast of Mexico that my mom and her sisters had discovered in the eighties and had been our holiday destination throughout my childhood. This trip was a turning point for Dad. A downturn. A turn for the worse. We were a great group: my uncle and his partner, my cousin and his girlfriend, my mom and dad. For the rest of us, that trip together was magical. We rode bikes through the little town, surfed the waves, drank margaritas at the Sunset Bar, and danced our tails off to Afro-Cuban renditions of classics such as "Candela" and "el Carretero" played by live bands at the Sand's pool bar.

My dad would wake up in the morning, take his amphetamines, which were the only way he could get enough juice to get up and go, and he'd ride his bike down the street to hit the courts with his pickleball paddle in hand. Pickleball was something that brought him great joy, and thanks to the amphetamines, he could still manage to play for a couple of hours in the morning, before the brain fog and fatigue set in. Of course, what goes up must come down, so he'd often have a serious energy crash in the afternoon, and the pills could give him anxiety and make it difficult for him to sleep. But if he had to choose between having a few hours where he could fully participate in something he loved, even if he had to pay the price, or never having enough energy to engage in any of the activities that made him happy, he'd have chosen participation.

I saw him zip out on the bike those mornings, looking sharp and alert, and it was easy to hang onto that image of him—active, mobile, agile. I didn't look his Parkinson's in the face until one morning when he told me that he wanted to take me out for breakfast. I had a little hangover because we had gone out dancing until late the night before, so when our lighthearted father-daughter breakfast on the balcony of Restaurante Bananas turned into a heart-to-heart conversation about his disease and his suffering, I could barely keep it together.

"Things are getting real," he said. "I'm missing out on everything. I can't engage in life the way I want to, and it kills me. I'm watching it go by, right there, right outside my room, but I can't even get up to join in. I'm locked inside this body that I can't control and inside this brain that shuts off, and who knows when it'll turn back on."

I blinked tears down my cheek. This was the first time I saw my dad start to buckle under the weight of his disease, and I couldn't bear it. His pain terrified me. I couldn't hold space for it. I didn't have space for it. It was too potent, too intense, too real.

Chapter 3
September 2020

My parents moved into the new house the September after Mexico. The idea of selling the farm had been casually tossed around over the previous year, but just like with everything else, I hadn't let it sink in. Apart from not being able to keep up with the maintenance of fifteen acres and three horses, my dad's worsening condition was making it almost dangerous for him to live so far outside of town, and they couldn't put it off any longer.

It broke his heart to have to leave the house that he'd so lovingly built. Broke it into a million guilt and shame-ridden pieces. It broke my mom's heart too, but she stepped up again and again to make the necessary sacrifices for my dad's wellbeing. She also knew that one day she'd be living alone in whichever house they occupied and being isolated out in the quiet countryside might not be the best option.

They had spent a few months doing repairs and sprucing the place up, and once it was on the market, it went fast. So fast, even, they didn't know where they were going to move yet. Mom mentioned the possibility of them moving into her sister's house while she was in Arizona seeking refuge from the oppressive Washington winters. They ended up buying a house from a friend who had moved into a condo. Although they didn't seem to love it, it was in town, it was easy, and they needed a place to live.

When I came back to Washington to help with the move, I put on my strongest emotional armor and most resilient smile to help them get through it, but I was devastated. I had spent my childhood on that farm, running around the forest, chasing fairies, building forts, and making potions out of flowers. I knew every inch of those woods—it had been my sanctuary. This was a place I would have the hardest time saying goodbye to, if I did indeed decide to let myself say goodbye. While we sifted through twenty-five years' worth of memories, I was steadfast in my commitment to dissociate in order to uphold the appearance of being strong, both for myself and for the others.

In a group effort between my two aunts, my cousin, my uncle, and my parents, and with the clock running out, we packed everything up, threw it into the moving vans, and took what we could to the new house. A week later, we turned in the keys.

"I thought we were gonna die in this house," my dad said to me on our last night at the farm. His eyes were red and bleary, and his voice quivered with heartbreak. "All the love and care I put into this place to make it your mom's dream home. And now she has to leave it behind and move into a shitty rambler with ugly cabinets."

We both cried quietly.

"I never in a million years would have imagined us leaving. We were supposed to grow old here," he said through his tears.

Chapter 4
May 2021

THE WHOLE YEAR AND A half after the trip to Mexico was a blur for my family, and for the whole world. The global health crisis took my attention off my dad's worsening condition, while at the same time, exacerbating his symptoms. The lack of social contact, the isolation, not being able to play pickleball, living in a continuous state of fear and anxiety due to the media's coverage of the pandemic—all of this contributed to pushing him over the edge.

Despite my preoccupation with the global pandemic, I did notice that our phone calls became shorter and less satisfying. They lasted as long as his head was in the game, which was typically between ten and fifteen minutes, and then he'd start to fade. But there was one conversation in May of 2021 that stood out.

We spoke for forty-five minutes, and he was alert and lucid the entire time. It was an achievement, felt like progress. I was so happy. I told him about a book that I had just read, *Many Lives, Many Masters* by Brian Weiss, and we got into a conversation about Buddhism and reincarnation. On the topic of dying, he mentioned his dear friend Lance who had died of brain cancer years before. He shared the realization that the joyous party Lance had thrown at his enchanted cabin in the woods shortly before his passing had actually been a farewell celebration, which he had organized because he'd known the end was near.

In that conversation, my dad told me about a Tedx Talk by a woman named Phyllis Shacter called "Not Here by Choice." She was from Bellingham, my hometown, and as it turned out, my dad had tuned their piano many years before. I think he saw a certain synchronicity in that. In the talk, she told the story of her husband who had chosen VSED, voluntarily stopping eating and drinking, as an end-of-life option to avoid having to live through the final stages of Alzheimer's. I thought we were just sharing, but in reality, my dad was priming me for a decision he was on the precipice of making.

A couple of weeks after that call, while making coffee one morning, I received an email. I opened it up and immediately felt my chest tighten. I gasped for air and went pale as a ghost. It was a message from my dad, with all of his family cc'd. Subject: *End of life choices*. He said that he was having a good deal more difficulty doing everyday tasks and that his quality of life was taking a dive. He was considering getting his ducks in a line. He thought VSED was the best option for him and wanted our two cents.

My mind raced a million miles a minute. My legs felt weak and wobbly. Thoughts such as *How could I not have seen this coming?* raced through my head. Of course, that conversation on the phone had meant something. There was a reason he'd been able to hold it together long enough to get through those forty-five minutes. He was giving me the message ahead of time, in his own way, so that I could be prepared for when the bomb dropped. Unfortunately, the mind often doesn't hear what it isn't ready to accept, and I was not ready to accept that my dad, my teacher, my lighthouse, my role model, was on his way off stage.

I raced over to snap open my laptop and started clicking away in a fury, searching for tickets from Málaga to Seattle the following week. I had to get there and get to the bottom of this. It wasn't something I could email back and forth about. I needed to see his face, touch his hands, look into his eyes. I needed to know if this was really happening, and if so, *when*.

Chapter 5
June 2021

THE PREMISE OF MY FIRST trip back to Washington at the beginning of June, after receiving that formidable email late May, was that the three of us were going to talk as a family about my dad's decision to do VSED when the time came. I didn't know what to expect or how to approach this conversation. I didn't have the skills for talking about death. We don't do that in my culture.

It was strange not going out to the farm, but they had made the new house cozy over the eight months since the move. My dad had his own room with an adjustable bed and a pulley system so he could get himself in and out of bed on his own. He also had his mechanical armchair that helped him to sit down and stand up with less effort. Those two places were where he spent most of his time. I'd gone with him to buy that chair on my previous visit, when we were moving them to their new home in the city. He'd handed me the keys to the truck like it was no big deal, but it was the first time in thirty-one years that he asked me to drive. It had destroyed me because I knew what it meant. His condition had hit a new milestone.

On my first evening home, we ordered some takeout. I plated everything up and set the table, just as we'd always done.

"Oh, are we eating at the table tonight?" my dad asked.

I looked at my mom, bewildered.

She told me under her breath that it was much easier for him to eat from the tray table at his chair in the living room, so that's what they'd been doing. I felt awful for not having known and for bringing attention to his limitations.

After he sat down, he asked me to bring him a glass of water.

When I set it down on the tray table, my mom came over with a little straw and nonchalantly dropped it in the glass. "He has trouble swallowing. The straws help," she whispered in my ear.

I couldn't believe how much I didn't know about my dad's condition and its decline. So much had changed since I'd last seen him just six months prior.

I glanced at him out of the corner of my eye from the couch. His fork was suspended in midair, about four inches from his open mouth, unmoving. He was so still it looked like a picture. I knew he was desperately begging his hand to move, but there wasn't enough dopamine to get the fork into his mouth. My heart sank into the pit of my stomach. He struggled to feed himself. When had this happened?

We didn't make many plans over the next few days. My dad was limited to the occasional breakfast outings and short walks around the park, because about midmorning, his brain fog usually started up. Even when we made those plans, sometimes they'd have to be canceled last minute because he'd had a bad night of body-anxiety and insomnia and could barely move or speak.

I was strong that first week, wanting to infuse him with strength and love, but also, I wasn't brave enough to go into the darkness and explore those deep caverns of pain and fear. Occasionally, my mom would mention that we all needed to talk, and I'd casually blow her off. "Definitely, but let's do it after I finish my online classes for the day," I'd say. And then when I'd finish teaching, she'd be at work or my dad would be in a brain fog. Finally, one day in the car on our way back from breakfast, he asked me if I had any questions for him. Of course I had questions, more than I could count, but I didn't have the words for any of them, nor the courage to find them.

I took a deep breath and decided it was time to face the beast. "I do. Can you just give me a little time to process?"

He nodded, and we drove home in heavy silence.

When we got back to the house, I took out a notebook and started writing down all of the questions that came to me.

Are you scared? What do you think will happen after you die? How will you make the decision about when to stop eating and drinking? Will a date be set in advance? Who will be here? How long will it take? Will there be a going away party? A ceremony? A funeral? What will happen to Mom? Who's going to make sure she's okay? Are we allowed to cry, or will that make it harder for you? What if you change your mind? What if you ask for a glass of water?

I was sitting next to him on the other armchair, and he read a book while I wrote. My mom was at work, and it was just the two of us.

He broke the silence when he saw my tears, cueing it was time to have the conversation. "How's the processing going?"

It felt safer to read everything through directly from the page, rather than lingering on each question and waiting for an answer. That way I had a better chance of getting through them without getting too emotional to continue.

After I powered through my list of questions, he sat in contemplation for a few moments and then began to answer. He told me that he was more afraid of making the decision too late than making it earlier than necessary. He said there were markers that would indicate how his quality of life was doing, and hitting those markers meant it was time—when he couldn't feed himself anymore, when he couldn't get in and out of bed, when he couldn't dress himself or go to the bathroom alone. He said that the night before he had hit one of his markers, he had woken up in the middle of the night and couldn't get out of bed. He was stuck laying there for hours, unable to call my mom and unable to lift his arm to ring his bell. That, for him, was not quality of life, and nor would it be for me.

He said that the hospice people would need a week's notice to get everything ready in the house and make sure things were set to go smoothly. He wanted my mom and me to be there, and any friends and family who wanted to sit with him. He requested a big, comfy chair in the bedroom so people could spend time with him reading and telling stories. He wanted music and laughter. There wouldn't be a celebration because his cognitive state was so unpredictable, and he would feel terrible if a party was planned that he later couldn't take part in. He didn't care about a funeral.

"Do what you want," he said. "I don't care what happens to my body. I won't be in it anymore. I'll be gone."

I wanted to know how I could communicate with him after he left. I wanted instructions, signs and symbols, an interdimensional language that would allow him to give me messages.

"If reincarnation means that my body decomposes and turns into dirt for a seed to grow, I'm happy with that."

His answer struck me as so material. I wanted something deeper from him, something metaphysical. I wanted to know where he thought his soul was going, the electricity that fires his brain synapses and runs his nervous system, his consciousness, his breath. What would happen to all of that? I knew deep down that it was going somewhere, but he surprised me by not having answers or even entertaining the questions. He was so trapped inside of that body that none of the other stuff mattered. He just wanted out. He just wanted to be free.

My life is infused with music thanks to my dad. I remember when he would set up his music stand and practice the recorder in his room every evening. He was always, if nothing else, dedicated to his passions and pragmatic in his approach. He would play classical guitar with a metronome, tinker on the piano, and had an incredible ear. There was always a soundtrack playing in the background of our lives.

When I was in elementary school, he started a band called Songo, in which he played the bass guitar. I remember that band well. His late friend Lance played percussion, along with another white-haired hippie named Eric. They had a sax player, who I thought was dreamy when I was ten years old. He was the youngster of the group. And there was a sweet flute player named Sage. This was at the height of my dad's "clave" phase. Clave is a rhythmic pattern used in the Afro-

Cuban jazz music they played, and it's what he lived and breathed during those years. Every song either had great clave or needed more clave, and any everyday object was a potential percussion instrument.

I have very fond memories of that band, even when their evening rehearsals in the garage, which shared a wall with my bedroom, would go late on school nights, and even when he and Lance would hang out just outside my bedroom window afterwards, smoking joints and making a commotion. Once, when the band members were all over at the house because they were going to play music at a big party my parents had thrown, I found a homemade pipe made out of a toilet paper roll and a bag of shake inside my Disney Princess pillowcase. I had climbed up into my treehouse to get a break from the party day chaos, and when I laid my head down, I noticed something bumpy underneath me. I knew what it was because a boy in my third-grade class had found something similar in the field next to the playground at recess. Someone in the band got a serious talking-to that day.

My dad had me taking piano lessons from when I was five years old all the way through elementary school. Sometimes I loved it, but I mostly resented it, especially as I got older. I hated the recitals, and I do believe that my performance anxiety stems partially from being forced to play the piano in front of groups of peers and parents when all I wanted to do was go climb the apple trees outside. I had to practice forty-five minutes every day after school, which felt like an eternity, especially because it coincided with my favorite after school TV show, *Saved by the Bell.* When my dad was out working in the field or fixing fences, I would sneak into the back room and turn on the TV with the volume down real low. When I heard him walking up the driveway, I'd quickly turn it off and scuttle back to the piano. He was none the wiser, which was lucky, because his temper was quick and explosive back then.

Despite my reluctance to pursue the piano, Dad and I always connected on a musical level. On my birthdays, he would give me handpicked CDs that were perfect for whatever phase of life I was in but were always something I would never have found on my own. He took me with him to the independent cinema to see a documentary on Buena Vista Social Club with Ry Cooder and Elias Ochoa, two of his musical idols. I even joined his eight-person marimba band for a summer and played with them in a concert at a music festival downtown.

My dad and I shared a lot of music with each other, but there's one song that reached me the deepest and created the strongest bond between us. It's an instrumental song called "Grant's Corner" on a bluegrass-country album by Jerry Douglas. On this particular track, the twang and patter of the typical hoedown bluegrass that I'd always heard was replaced with the slow and haunting melancholic beauty of Mark O'Connor's violin and Jerry Douglas's Dobro guitar. Every time I hear this song, it changes me.

He first played it for me when I was a young child, and I called it the "whale song" because the sorrowful melody reminded me of the sea and the sound of whales calling through the deep. He'd told me then that he imagined this song playing at his wake.

Through the sorrow, there's also a kindness and a softness that stirs you up but which simultaneously brings in a sense of peace.

During my first visit in June, he'd told me that he had a theory about music. He was sitting in his electric armchair, where he spent the majority of his day, and I was sitting next to him on the couch. We had just listened to the whale song.

"It's not a sad song, but it's enveloping," he'd said slowly and softly, never in a hurry when expressing himself. "I was trying for years to figure it out, but then I realized, while listening to and experiencing songs that really struck me, that certain music is, for lack of a better word, *inevitable*. It's like the essence is almost independent of the author or the time. When you hear a song like that, it's like, how could it be anything else? How could it be that it wasn't meant to be? This is one of those songs."

We'd sat with that for a moment before he continued, "The muse—artists, musicians, authors, they've all talked about how it just comes. It wasn't a chore, but it was almost a blessing. Like it was channeled from somewhere else. Like it already existed before they created it, or it's even somehow existed forever. That's why I thought of the word *inevitable*."

Chapter 6

I HADN'T THOUGHT MUCH ABOUT DEATH until it got close enough for me to feel its breath. My dad hadn't had any answers that satisfied me about where we go when we die and where we've been before we were born, and those questions kept churning around inside me. My childhood friend, Miette, comes from a spiritual family and was my first connection to esoteric and spiritual exploration, and her mom, Michelle, studied hypnotherapy. She'd asked me once if she could practice on me by trying out a dream regression. It had been a fascinating and positive experience, but one which I never pursued further. While I was asking Dad all of these questions that had never occurred to me before, I thought of Michelle and of our regression ten years prior. Could she help me find answers? So, I asked her if she'd be willing to dust off her hypnosis skills and try a past life regression, and she responded enthusiastically. A few days after the unsettling conversation with my dad, I drove toward the lake to her house, to see if I could scratch some layers and get some clarity.

I laid down on the bed and closed my eyes, ready for anything but expecting nothing. Michelle started by bringing me to a garden in my imagination, my special place, where the delicate floral notes of Jasmine tiptoed on the warm afternoon breeze. And then, the journey began.

"Now, you are going to take a journey through time," she said calmly.

Completely relaxed and with my eyes closed, I felt my entire body sinking backward, as if it were moving through space and time. Michelle brought me to the ground, where I saw a door with a glowing emerald doorknob. I reached out to open it and walked through the door, into an unknown place.

"What do you see?" she asked.

But I saw nothing. I was surrounded by fog. I waited patiently, and the fog began to lift, from which an expansive prairie emerged. In the distance, I could see some rolling hills, and behind me and to the right there were trees—the beginning of a wooded area. "I'm in a field," I said. I noticed a heaviness in my body and in my energy. I didn't feel like explaining details, so I only communicated the minimum for Michelle to follow along. "I have two long braids," I said, noticing that I was looking at myself from behind now, instead of through my eyes. I was sitting on my knees surrounded by a brownish-gold colored steppe landscape.

"Can you see what you're wearing?" Michelle asked.

I couldn't.

"Look down at your feet. Are you wearing shoes?"

I was almost surprised to see that I could, in fact, see my shoes. They were made of leather and looked like a type of moccasin. Then I said a phrase that I would repeat again and again throughout the regression. It came out in a breathy whisper, on the exhale, after taking in a deep breath. "I'm just resting." Another deep inhale. "I just need to rest." I didn't feel physically tired like one would after having walked a long distance or having done a physically demanding task. I felt like my body and my mind were heavy, like I was low on life energy, and I truly just needed to rest.

I saw a small basket next to me filled with leaves that looked similar to dried bay leaves but slightly bigger. "I've been collecting these leaves," I told Michelle. "There's a woman of my people who's ill. She's very old." I took a deep breath. "I need to boil these leaves and place them on her forehead."

At this moment, something incredible happened. I became aware of three separate beings, or consciousnesses, that were all happening at the same time. There was the woman from the regression whose thoughts and feelings I was experiencing. Then there was "Kate," who for some reason I perceived to the right of me and who was quietly skeptical of everything happening. And then there was me, my essence, who was observing everything unfold, who made the decision to speak or not to speak, who was aware of my body, the bed I was on, and Michelle's voice, but who was also aware of Kate's skeptical comments, and of the thoughts and feelings of the woman in the regression.

And then, from inside the mind of the woman, I saw the elder. Just like you can imagine your mother's face, the woman imagined this elder, and I could see her clearly. She had rough, weatherworn skin and bushy, shoulder-length hair that was a blend of dark gray and stark white. She was the shamanic healer of the community. I understood that my boiling the leaves and placing them on her head would not be an attempt to heal her, but rather would serve as a passing ritual, helping her to release her body and transition into another spiritual plane. I felt a deep love and respect for this woman. She was my teacher and my existential guide.

"She is *Nanai*." I didn't know what it meant, but I said it regardless.

I just needed to rest. I knew they were waiting for me, but I also knew that nothing would happen until I returned and carried out the ceremony. If I went back before I was ready, before I had rested and recovered the necessary energy, I would not be able to do the ritual the way it was meant to be done. My heart ached.

I looked out over the shortgrass prairie and an amazing feeling came over me. "I understand everything. Nothing is foreign." This was all I could say to Michelle to explain the incredible understanding that had just washed over me. It was an understanding that I felt in the marrow of my bones, in the blood in my veins, in the air in my lungs. I saw how everything was connected. I *knew* each blade of grass, each cloud, each insect.

Everything had a purpose. Everything made sense. *Nothing was foreign.* I felt completely at home in a way that I never had before. But this woman lived with this understanding. It was integrated into her very nature.

After some time, I looked out to my left and saw a wolf approaching me. I was curious but unafraid. When she got closer, I realized that I knew her. She was my friend. "She's here to support me," I said, and a tear fell from my eye—my real, physical eye on my real, physical body.

The wolf sat down next to me and put her massive, gray head on my shoulder, which filled me with an overwhelming love that was so powerful I felt like I was going to burst. I reached out and put my hand on her head, and I could feel the coarse fur between my fingers. She shook her head playfully, and I laughed out loud.

As I sat with this majestic creature, who towered over me in my seated position, I began to whisper out loud, but this whisper didn't come from my awareness. I was speaking as the woman to the wolf, and although the sounds I was making weren't from a language I recognized, I knew that I was telling her I loved her and thanking her for her loyalty and support. At this point, the other Kate began to feel uncomfortable with all of this.

"Michelle's going to think you're crazy," she thought. But I just shrugged her away and kept whispering what must have sounded like nonsense but what I knew carried deep meaning.

Throughout the regression, starting the moment I walked through the door with the emerald doorknob, my physical body had been trembling. It became more and more intense, until the convulsions were similar to those of a seizure. I knew Michelle would be starting to worry and want to bring me back soon.

Feeling the strength given to me by the wolf, I stood up and picked up the basket. It was time for me to make the journey back to my people, back to *Nanai*. I began walking toward the trees, and Michelle told me that my trip back in time was coming to a finish. She guided me back to my garden and counted me back into an awake state, but when I opened my eyes, something was off. I felt fractured, spread out, like I wasn't totally contained within my body. I was twitchy and awkward and didn't talk like myself. After a few minutes, we walked out into the kitchen where my friend was waiting, and I still felt off.

"My blood sugar," was all I could say.

Michelle whipped me up some lemonade, and I sipped it as she recounted the story for Miette. I listened carefully as Michelle described the experience from her perspective, and I was moved by how deeply it had affected her as well.

"And the interesting thing," she said with wide eyes and a smile, "was that at one point you started whispering a language that wasn't Spanish or English."

After roughly half an hour, something snapped into place. All of a sudden, I was able to talk normally again, and I was no longer twitching. "Woah, that was weird. I'm back now though!" I said, laughing from my perch at the counter.

I knew that I had just been given an incredible gift, but it was too soon to fully take it in. I needed time. A whole unseen world had just been opened up to me. Something told me that the answers to the questions I had been asking were woven into that experience and I would have to tease them out, but at the time, I felt equally as confused as I felt reassured.

I tried to go about my day as normal, but even as I went through the usual steps, they felt awkward and mechanical. I had witnessed something that had shaken me to my core. Even though I had been open to these ideas of past lives and alternate timelines, to be given even a minuscule taste of what else could exist beyond our bodies, beyond our minds, caused me to deeply question the framework of what I believed. How could I go about my day, business as usual, after such an experience?

I was desperate to share with the people closest to me my journey to another dimension, but at the same time, reluctant, recognizing that hearing such accounts could only affect a person to a certain degree before doubt laid its boundary. I wanted to protect my discovery from skepticism and mockery as much as I wanted to share it.

The next day, after what I thought to be an appropriate amount of time for integration, I tried sharing the experience with my dad but was met with exactly what I'd feared most—indifference. I wanted him to care about this as much as I did, be as inspired as I was, and want to spend whatever time he had left solving the riddle with me. But he was not in that space. Didn't he see that this was my attempt to find peace in his imminent passing? His indifference hit me like a personal rejection, and my heart sank in my chest. But I was looking at it too closely. The magic held in that regression didn't need external validation in order to unfold.

Chapter 7

When my aunt Lulu and my uncle Howard came to pick me up to drive the two hours to the airport in Seattle, my dad made the effort to walk down the steep driveway to the road and see me off. I knew it killed him not to be able to help me with my suitcases like he had always done. He gave me two kisses on the cheek, and his scratchy gray beard tickled my skin. When I reached around to give him a hug, I had a feeling. I call it a "download," but it's a form of intuition when you suddenly just *know* something. I knew that the very next time I saw him, I'd be saying goodbye, and I knew it wouldn't be too long from then.

In the car, the three of us talked about my mom. She is a veterinarian with her own clinic, a lifelong horse enthusiast, and a skilled gardener. She's always got something she needs to do—swing by work, go out and visit her horse at the stables where she's boarding him, walk the dog, work on the wild hill next to the house that she's taming into a beautiful garden, cleaning the house, running errands, and all of that on top of the myriad of things she was doing to take care of Dad. I worry that when she does finally slow down, everything will catch up with her all at once. The thing is, no one can prevent her from falling, but we can be there to catch her when she does.

When I finally arrived back in Spain, I let out a deep sigh of relief. As awful as it felt to leave them behind, I knew I needed to take care of myself. Those weeks in Bellingham had asked so much of me. Watching my parents go through all of that while fully stepping into their world was both shocking and heartbreaking. I didn't have the skills or tools to truly sink into and share my emotional experience at the time, so I ended up doing a lot of self-regulating and dissociating in order to be a source of positivity for my family. Throw jet lag in the mix, and I was completely depleted. I needed to spend some time recovering. I needed to replenish my reserves.

Seeing my dog felt like the warmest hug around my heart. I slept twelve hours that night, and the next day we spent a marvelous and healing summer afternoon at the beach. The Mediterranean water cleansed me of my energetic aches and pains and the sun recharged me. That Sunday evening, I received news from my mom. She said that after I left on Friday, my dad had had an episode. They spent two nights in the hospital because he wasn't able to move or swallow. I needed to return.

I called the airlines to see if I could change the tickets that I had for September, which was when I had originally planned to visit, and my earliest option was July 4, a week away. My mom's response was clear and stark. *Get new tickets. Get here ASAP.*

I felt panic flood my veins as adrenaline shot through my system. Was he dying right now? Was I going to miss it? I spent the next couple of hours searching for flights, but nothing was working out. I'd either have to take a seven hour overnight bus to Madrid and then wait through two five-hour layovers, resulting in a forty-hour journey, or fly out from where I lived in Málaga a day later and spend a night in Amsterdam. And when was I going to get the PCR test that would allow me to get on the airplane? I needed an appointment for that. And how long would the results take to get in? My tears splattered on the keyboard of my laptop.

"We can't solve this tonight," Alex said at 3 a.m. "You need to sleep. Let's go to bed, and tomorrow, when all of the offices are open, we'll find a solution. At 8 a.m. sharp, we'll be here making phone calls, I promise, but right now you need to rest."

He was right. My relationship had been struggling, and I didn't feel connected to him, but I did appreciate that reflection and support. I fell into bed and released myself into a deep and undisturbed sleep.

The next morning, as we were driving to the airport to get my PCR test, I had a sudden realization. Just like the woman in my regression had needed to rest before joining her tribe for the passing ritual of her teacher, *so had I*. If I took that insane, forty-hour journey, I would arrive in Seattle in a million broken pieces and wouldn't be of any use to anyone. But if I rested and gathered my strength, I could be of service. I realized that it made no sense to race home in fear of my father leaving before I got there, if it meant that I would be bringing with me a load of exhaustion and heavy energy. I needed to arrive in one piece, so that I could support him. And if I arrived late, I could be there for my mom, because she was going to need the strongest, healthiest, and most loving version of me. For the first time since I had learned about my dad's decline, I was able to relax my shoulders and take a full, deep breath.

I bought a ticket for a flight out of Málaga on Wednesday afternoon, giving me two days to rest and prepare. For my overnight layover in Amsterdam, I booked a hotel room so that I could sleep comfortably and continue my journey the following day. I never would have given myself this luxury if it weren't for the wisdom I'd received in the regression.

Those two days were a blur. I spent most of my time moving very little and feeling a lot, either on the beach being held by the sun and the sea, or on the couch holding my dog. When the time came to leave again, I wasn't entirely healthy, but I was a little less sleep-deprived and could feel that my nervous system had been soothed by the medicine of the Mediterranean and my furry best friend. Packing was a journey, because I had no idea how long I'd be gone or what would be required of me, and it broke my heart to say goodbye to my dog Laila, who had supported me through everything over the past four years. But I had to go.

I left the airport in Amsterdam and dropped my bags off at the hotel down the street, in an industrial area. Since my dad's family comes from the Netherlands and I've visited many times, Amsterdam is a significant place for me. I really wanted to embrace this idea of self-care, so I decided to take a bus into the city. It seemed ridiculous to be out sightseeing while my dad was potentially dying, but I did my best and tried to do it in his honor, as Amsterdam was also very dear to his heart. I walked along the canals under the cloudy, oppressive sky and visited my favorite corners of the city, taking it all in. I treated myself to Vietnamese pho, which didn't exist where I lived in Spain, and I allowed myself to be deeply nourished and comforted.

Walking by the *I Amsterdam* sculpture, I felt a sharp pain. The last time I had been in Amsterdam was with Dad, when Mom and I brought him to the "homeland" for the first and only time. My favorite picture from that trip was of my parents standing between the letters of that sculpture, their faces full of joy and childlike wonder. It felt meaningful to be there, of all places, taking my layover on this specific journey. I could feel his presence everywhere.

Chapter 8
July 1, 2021 – The Last Meal

I HAD KNOWN THAT VSED, VOLUNTARILY stopping eating and drinking, was on the table for my dad as an end-of-life option, but when I left my family in Bellingham, Washington to return to where I lived in Spain just a week before, I had thought we still had time. We all did. Maybe six months. Maybe a year. Maybe two. When I got back on a plane, urgently summoned by my mom, I knew something was wrong, but I didn't know exactly what the situation was. It wasn't until I arrived at the Seattle airport from Amsterdam, after flying across the Atlantic Ocean for the second time within a week, that I found out my dad would be starting his end-of-life journey the following day.

I was in the car with my cousin, Dylan, who had picked me up from the airport, and we were making the two-hour drive to Bellingham. When I called my mom to check in and let her know I was on my way, she told me, "You know your dad is preparing to start his fast? He thinks he's going to start tomorrow."

I remember feeling completely caught off guard, like I had been left in the dark about possibly the most important thing that's ever happened. But the truth was that she had no idea what was going on either. We were all at the whim of the sudden progression of his disease.

His siblings had traveled from Michigan after hearing about his health crisis during the week I was back in Spain and were all at the house when I arrived. When I walked up the lawn toward the front door, they greeted me with tired faces and heavy hearts. They had been crying. They had just finished a family meeting together to talk about the end-of-life process my dad was about to undertake and what that would mean for everyone.

We were all in emotional shock. We bumbled around the kitchen and the living room, bumping into each other, trying to divvy up tasks to prepare his last-minute requests for his last meal before he began what he's been calling "The Final Fast." Marionberry and apple pies with lots of vanilla ice cream. The gouda cheese I had bought in Amsterdam during my layover. A bottle of Vouvray. An American Spirit cigarette.

He pulled me aside and asked if I'd make a trip to the gas station to get the cigarettes, and when I procured the unopened pack of blue Spirits from my suitcase, his eyes lit up.

"I knew you'd ask for one," I said. When I had packed my bags, I didn't know he'd be starting VSED, but I did know something serious was going on. He'd always been a repressed smoker, so I figured I should come prepared. No one else in the family would consider buying cigarettes, I was sure, so it was my duty.

We were sitting out on the front porch watching the sunlight slowly start to fade away. The picturesque July sunsets in Northwest Washington linger on until late in the evening before slowly transitioning into nightfall. He took a sip of his wine from the little straw that he's used since his trouble swallowing began. As he slowly pulled the cigarette up to his lips, one of his sisters walked by and made a grimace of disapproval.

"What?" he said, with a sly smile and that mischievous twinkle that makes his blue eyes pop. "It's not like it's gonna kill me."

A trickster with intention. No, Dad. That pack of cigarettes is not going to kill you.

Chapter 9
July 2, 2021 – The Final Fast: Day One

I woke up the next day and couldn't stop thinking about how the next room over, my dad was slowly ending his life. I'd first woken up at five o'clock in the morning, and as soon as I'd opened my eyes, I felt my stomach drop, like I had just fallen off a ledge. My body was confused by all of the time-zone jumping I'd been doing, and the emotional and physical exhaustion was catching up with me.

There were already noticeable changes in his health and behavior. He'd stopped taking his Parkinson's medication the night before, and because of that and the dehydration, his tremors were much more noticeable. Andrea, our death doula who spoke with a soft breathiness and had eyebrows that were tilted perpetually upwards in a show of compassion, explained to us that even just a tablespoon of water is enough to keep his kidneys running for three days. She brought over a spray bottle that sprayed a mist so fine we wouldn't have to worry much about overdoing it when he asked us to moisten his mouth. Ultimately, we had to keep his goal in mind and refrain from doing anything to prolong the already difficult process he was going through.

He had visitors over late morning. His best friend Tony, who helped build the farmhouse, and Tony's wife, Susan, came by. We sat out on the deck under the shade of the umbrella, my dad in his wheelchair because he was already too weak to support himself. I acted as his interpreter. I could pick up the weak, whispery dance of words when he spoke if I quieted my mind and put my ear close to his mouth. I often knew what he was saying just through intuition, while others had to ask him to repeat again and again.

Tony took my dad's now-delicate hand and told him how much he loved him. Through the tears, I listened closely and helped them communicate. He told Tony about the whale song, but Tony hadn't heard it before.

"Why don't we have a listen," my dad whispered to me.

I went to the living room and got the wooden speaker he'd used to play music outside. With the first soulful notes of the violin, Tony's eyes cascaded with tears. The song echoed throughout the house and the yard, and as if it were a gathering call, the others—my dad's brother and sisters, my cousin Monika, and my mom's sister Lulu—came one by one and joined us at the table. No one spoke. No one made eye contact. We were all somewhere far away, each of us in a different place, a sad and tender place of recognition that this was Dad's way of bidding us farewell.

The rest of the day floated by as we all tried to find our roles in this production. There were more logistical details to hash out than I had realized, things like coordinating visits and time spent with him, food preparation, and general hospice caretaking. I set up a table in the garage and moved the microwave, water pitcher, a cooler for drinks, and all of the random snacks that people had brought over to the house out there, so that he wouldn't see, hear, or smell any evidence of eating or drinking. We had to be militant about not bringing any triggers into his room. I put a sign on the front door that read:

> *Before coming inside, please put your hand on your heart and take a deep*

breath in. Breathe in love, and breathe it back out. You are about to enter a safe and sacred space. Respectfully leave any food or drink items in the garage. Thank you, and Namaste.

That evening, my mom organized the caretaking night shifts because he needed his low dose of morphine and levodopa squirted under his tongue every couple of hours in order to stay comfortable. Someone had to be with him at all times, and there were no available caretakers in Bellingham or the surrounding areas. His decision was so quick that we weren't able to take care of many of the preparations. It felt like we were just throwing this thing together.

There was so much different energy around the house. The Michigan family was staying at a hotel, but when they came over in the morning, and Mom's side of the family, whom I'd grown up with, were there as well, all of this energy got mixed up and muddled around. It stuck to me and seeped into me, and I didn't know what was mine and what wasn't.

My friend Katie was driving up from Seattle to see him on the next day, bringing her fourteen-year-old Chihuahua and her newly adopted puppy. I met Katie on a study-abroad trip to

Spain over ten years ago, and she became part of the family over the years. My mom calls her "Second Daughter." She and I share one of my most precious memories of my dad. We'd taken a family vacation together with my parents to Isla de Mujeres off the coast of Mexico nine years ago, and it had been a magical week of sun, sand, and margaritas. On a Sunday evening, the four of us climbed into a golf cart and took a joy ride around the island. Katie was the driver, my mom the copilot, and my dad and I sat in the back. As we cruised through the town, my dad blasted Bob Marley and the Wailers at full volume on his portable wooden speaker with a big smile on his face. We'd been quite the crew. Nothing majorly eventful happened, but it was the quality of the moment that left such a strong memory. We were all so present, so embodied in ease and enjoyment and open to the experience of being with each other, just as we were. Driving around as the sun set, listening to reggae, laughing—there was a feeling of pure acceptance and receptivity to life that we all felt and have spoken about ever since.

I was looking forward to her visit. Everything she does is just so Katie, which is beautiful, because it means that she knows herself and is herself. She brings laughter wherever she goes, delivered with the beauty and class of her favorite Tiffany & Co. earrings and an irreverence that my dad appreciated deeply. Her career as an oncology nurse often left her emotionally depleted and in need of care and support, which are things I am always honored to give her, but this time, I needed her to be the caregiver and knew she was up for the task.

Chapter 10
Day Two

THE BERGAMOT ESSENTIAL OILS I'D been putting in the diffuser helped to keep the air from feeling too heavy with all the tears that had fallen, continued to fall, in this room. It was nighttime, and the house was still. The room was only lit by the flickering flame of the angel candle that Katie brought for him and put on the dresser next to the many vases of flowers friends and family had sent. His breathing was soft, and his movements were rare and slow. I was sitting on the side of his bed, longing for him to tell stories or share wisdom, but he didn't have the energy to engage.

Every minute that went by was a minute closer to his exit, and I felt the pressure to tie up all of the loose ends before he left. It felt like now or never. I didn't want to regret not asking him all of those deep and soulful questions about his life and his memories, but this wasn't about me. It was not about me being a daughter or him being a father. It was about a tired soul who didn't want to suffer anymore. This was his process, and he was the one who needed to feel that his loose ends were tied up.

"I'd love to keep learning from you over my entire life," I whispered. His eyes were halfway open, but I don't know if he could hear me or if he was in a deep, morphine slumber. "But all the real work you had to do with me has already been done."

A light summer breeze was coming in through the window, causing the shadow flowers to dance on the wall. Although I'd been crying on and off all day, right then my eyes were dry—I wanted him to feel my strength, not my pain.

"I respect and admire you for what you're doing, and I wouldn't expect anything less of you after the life of dignity and intention that you've lived." I looked him deep in the eyes and took his clenched and fragile hand between mine. "You can go in peace."

"You're too much," he whispered.

A tear dropped from my eye, onto his chest.

Chapter 11
Day Three

I WONDERED HOW MANY MORNINGS IT would take for me to get used to waking up in this full, yet silent house. Obviously, more than three. Katie and I shared my bed that night. She brought so much love with her, and I don't know how she did it, but she also brought joy. She loved my dad, and I knew this was heartbreaking for her too, but she was stepping up for us, for my mom and I. She was not doing what she needed but what love needed, and I love her for it.

For the last sixteen hours, I'd gotten to see one of my closest friends do what she is a natural at, and highly trained to do, which is taking care of people. I'd never seen her in her professional environment, but watching the care that she took with my dad when giving him his medicine, checking his vitals, repositioning him, I was in awe of her gentleness and grace. Her alarm went off every two hours last night, waking her up to give my dad his morphine, which she'd volunteered to do. I was so glad that no one was asking me to do it. I don't know if I could have handled it.

I was in the room with him, and he was very still. I'd been reading him some poems by James Wright, whom I knew he liked, but I was not sure if he was in the mood to hear them. I put some music on, but I didn't know what he wanted to listen to. There was nothing like having a DJ who couldn't read the room and not being able to ask her to change the track.

Am I allowed to say that I want him to go? I thought. It's not like I was wishing death upon my father—he was the one choosing to die—but just wishing that he got his wish. I wanted him to let go so that we could let go, because every day the rope we were holding on to got thinner, and I struggled to keep my grip on it and on my own sanity.

Later that day, I glanced outside and saw Sue and Dennis getting out of their car, guitar and flute in one hand, music stand and flowers in the other. Sue's face was somehow still lit up by her beautiful smile even though this one carried a distinct heaviness.

Michael and Rosanne were there too. I watched them from Dad's bedroom window as they awkwardly rounded up the instruments and made their way to the front door. How could one not be awkward in a situation like that? They had come to play songs to their beloved bandmate and best friend, who had chosen this week to die.

The Saddle Bums they called themselves. They'd been playing old country songs and other cowboy classics together for years—since before his diagnosis, in fact. Not only did they play music together, but they also shared a passion for horses. The six of them had gone on epic horseback-riding adventures in the mountains and through the redwoods, and hearing stories of their adventures gave me admiration and reverence for their love and loyalty to each other. Dennis and Sue had taken my dad and I out on their sailboat a few summers ago. They'd cracked out the whiskey and the guitars as the sun was setting over the San Juan Islands, and their soul friendship danced over the water to melodies of John Prine and the Beatles.

As my dad's disease took away his dexterity—slowly at first, and then in the blink of an eye, he was asking me to open the jar of peanut butter for him—he became unable to play the guitar. Don't, however, think for a second that it stopped him from playing music—his Scorpio determination and drive would never allow him to give up on something he was that passionate about without first exhausting every other alternative. As a solution to his lack of agility, he bought himself a dobro. This type of slide guitar rests on your lap and requires much less dexterity in the left hand, his weaker one, than a normal guitar, and it got him through for a number of years. When his voice began to fade, he started setting up a microphone for himself when they played their informal gigs at their friends' summer parties. He mostly did backup vocals and harmonies, but "If I Had a Boat" by Lyle Lovett was the one tune for which he took the lead and held it the whole way through. His Frisian roots gave him his love of horses and the sea, and his time in the Southwest nurtured his cowboy spirit. That song touched all of those pieces of him.

I got up and rushed outside to welcome the heavy-hearted band. Hugs were exchanged, and we recognized and honored each other's pain with a soulful greeting. They'd come with deep grief and brimming with love and wanted to sing and strum that love into music for my dad. I told them they could set up in the yard, in front of the deck. I was excited to tell Dad about his visitors.

"Dad, the Bums are here to play music for you!" I whispered as I gently squeezed his shoulder.

His reaction, or lack thereof, confused me. He had said he wanted people telling him stories, playing music, and laughing. Tears were okay, but he didn't want the constant solemnity that death usually carries. This time with him wasn't supposed to feel like a funeral. He had said he wanted levity, lightheartedness, a celebration.

"I don't want to see anyone right now." His words come out breathy and difficult to decipher.

I didn't understand. This was so different from the image he had painted for us. Nothing about this felt light or jovial. "Should I tell them to wait, or just start playing outside?"

"I don't care."

The band set up and started playing, but morale was down after the rejection they'd just received. All of the stragglers around the house—God there were so many of us—were drawn to the deck by the music. We tapped our feet to the songs the Saddle Bums had been playing for us for years, under very different circumstances, and some of us were even able to get out of our heads enough to sing along.

I told my mom about my confusion, and she explained the situation with the catheter. It wasn't working correctly and was causing him noticeable discomfort, but due to some physiological function he felt as though he constantly needed to go to the bathroom but couldn't get up and down on his own anymore, so going to the toilet was a whole ordeal. She said that the situation had him pretty twisted up.

After a couple of songs, I walked back to his room to check on him. I opened the door and could instantly feel the density in the room.

"How are you, Dad. Do you want to come out?"

"Shut the window," he whispered. He didn't have the strength even for a please or a thank you. He was suffering.

I closed the window and walked back outside, with an ocean of grief filling my heart. Hearing the songs that he had lovingly selected and learned for the band of best friends and not being able to play with them was too painful for him. One of his greatest joys that he'd never experience again in this lifetime was being thrown right in his face. Theirs was a gesture of pure love and camaraderie that now, in a different light, seemed careless and insensitive. It was disheartening how impossible it felt to know the right way to be in this completely uncharted territory.

I went back outside and looked around at the people sitting on the deck and on the lawn, scanning their faces. We were all lost and far away, and at the same time, so completely present for this. The last time we'd all been together, including the Michigan family, was at my wedding, and before then I have no idea.

Aunt Lulu stepped out of the kitchen onto the deck, after checking on my dad, and whispered to me that he wanted to come outside. I squealed and squeezed Monika's arm. She then jumped up, always eager and willing to help out however she can, and went back to the bedroom with Lulu to get him up and into his wheelchair. A song or two later, she wheeled him onto the porch like royalty, and we lit up with cheer and applause.

He smiled, but didn't speak, and I held his hand as we listened, squeezing it occasionally to the beat. When "If I Had a Boat" came on and they sang his solo, quiet tears rolled down my face. I knew it was pouring down rain in his heart too.

The evening of Day Three of the fast was the Fourth of July, and people were celebrating with the usual fireworks displays. Out there, they were eating hot dogs, drinking beer, barbecuing, laughing. We existed in a bubble. This house had a forcefield around it, an energetic casing that kept us separate from the "out there." What was happening in there was sacred, transcendental, and the only thing that mattered.

I felt like I was moving through a cloud. Everything was slowed down, and the sounds around me were muted. I felt drunk on a hot and hazy summer heaviness, but the bite of impending death was sobering.

Everyone sat on the deck watching the explosions of color light up the sky over Bellingham Bay. I observed the backs of their heads through the living room window, unable to conceive of anything happening outside of those walls. My dad was in the bedroom, slowly dying, and it was the only thing that was real.

Chapter 12
Day Four

I SIFTED THROUGH THE TINY PIECES splayed out over the table, as if completing this puzzle would make it all make sense. My uncle, Howard, was at the other side of the table with his back to the sun, and he was even more focused than me. I looked up at my dad in his wheelchair, his elbows bent and his hands clasped awkwardly together at chest level. His eyes were glassy and strikingly blue, like they were being illuminated from within. He was now completely stiff, and it was difficult to make out what he wanted to say, even for me. Nearly impossible.

I played some cello music for him that morning, and Ludovico Einaudi in the afternoon, which he must have liked because it made him want to come outside. It was a very exciting moment when he was able to almost telepathically communicate with me that he wanted to sit on the deck with us.

I raced outside to tell my aunt, "Dad wants out. He wants to get up!"

She jumped out of her chair, and we got him into the wheelchair as quickly and gracefully as possible, which is not an easy task when the person being moved can't assist in the effort. I rolled him outside onto the deck, and everyone cheered.

Now, after all of that adrenaline and commotion, there we were, sifting through puzzle pieces in silence, hoping that the sun felt good on his skin.

That morning when I woke up, I'd heard music coming out of his room. It was Agnes's first night with him. She was a kindhearted woman in her seventies who came from Kenya, whom my mom had hired as a night caretaker for Dad. Agnes had the most joyful eyes, and a sly smile that, in a way, reminded me of his. She had put some music on her phone for him to listen to, but he couldn't tell her what he liked, so she'd had to guess.

When she left the room, I'd slinked in, freshly rolled out of bed. It was early, and I didn't hear anyone else moving around the house. I laughed to myself that Agnes had chosen country-pop music to play for him. It wouldn't have been his first choice, nor his second.

"Poor guy, couldn't get away if you tried," I'd whispered in his ear, and he'd smiled.

Moments like that told me that he was still in there. But why? What was he holding on to? Looking at him shriveled up in his wheelchair, weak and unable to move, I had to remind myself that he'd chosen this way, knowing that he would suffer. We couldn't take on that suffering, and we couldn't take it away from him either. This was his.

He'd told me during one of our bizarre, yet normalized conversations about the dying process that the reason he chose not to use chemicals to end his life was because he could see himself swallowing the pill and then having a flash of fear or doubt or regret. He'd said he didn't want fear to be the last emotion he experienced before leaving this earth. The depth of that insight pulled me in.

Chapter 13
Day Five

On Day Two, Katie, an experienced oncology nurse at one of Seattle's finest hospitals, said that he looked much farther along than she had expected. On Day Four, Tiffany, the hospice nurse, had said that things were moving very quickly and we could expect just a day or two more of this. Andrea was also impressed by his rapid "progression." But I asked the pendulum, and it said that he was scared and still wasn't ready to let go. What was going through his mind? It haunted me that there was no way to know.

It was still early. I didn't sleep well. When I first got up, I was angry and caught myself making uncharacteristically snide remarks. Realizing it, I had to check myself. Where was the anger coming from? After sitting with it for a few minutes, it did what anger often does for me. It lowered its fangs, dropped its weapons, and turned into a deep, blue ocean of sadness that engulfed me and dragged me down into its depths. I was there right then. I was angry that he didn't think to leave me one final piece of wisdom, that he hadn't prepared a last loving message for me, his only daughter, before starting to let go. Now, connection with him looked like a twitch of his tongue, a grunt, a hand squeeze, but I never really knew what to think. I started to read into it, thinking he was trying to tell me something, and then he had some muscle spasm that made me feel stupid for thinking that any of this was actually about me.

I could feel myself putting him on a pedestal on his last dying days and saw how that could be dangerous. I certainly hadn't always had him there. It wasn't until the last seven years that I started truly seeing his softness and grace, which I'm sure had always been there. But he also had a temper. And the venom of a scorpion's tail in his tongue, which stung like a million shards of broken glass piercing every inch of my five-year-old body.

Maybe the deep-ocean sadness came from knowing that I'd never get the apology I'd always yearned for.

With Intention

A few hours after those big emotions that morning, something incredible happened. I was listening to an album by Beautiful Chorus and feeling the smooth surface of a heart-shaped amethyst that I cradled in my palm. It was a token from a dear family friend, sent along with flowers and a card. I had been meditating with it, finding a bit of calm and comfort in the cool weight in my hands, when I had a realization.

This was a gift that Dad was intentionally giving us. In stopping his Parkinson's treatment, he was showing us what he'd been fighting against all those years. He was allowing us to see him, to accompany him, and inviting us to understand. He was giving us the time, which we may not have wanted or ever imagined we needed, to experience his disease with him and grieve alongside him. He was giving us the opportunity not only to witness but to experience with him one of the most important moments of his life—his death. This was a deeply compassionate gift.

I noticed the contrast between the way my body felt with those thoughts and the way I'd felt earlier that morning. I was lighter, and my heart felt more open.

Tiffany, the young hospice nurse, was there. I could hear the perky up-tones of her voice from across the house, which were disorienting in conversations about palliative care. I heard her coming down the hallway, then a light tap on my bedroom door nudged it open.

"Kate, I just want to make sure you're getting the time with your dad that you need. There are a lot of people here, and there's a lot of coming and going, and I know it can be hard to have time alone with him."

I nodded my head slowly, but I was expressionless.

"I would just hate for you to regret not having the chance to tell him anything before he goes. It's going to happen soon." She gave me a warm smile and closed the door.

Now what? What do I do with that? Have I told him everything? I know he doesn't have any last words, at least none that he can express. But do I? I pulled out my journal and began to write. What came out was his eulogy.

Eulogy

My dad is the trickster, the quiet careful listener
who hears the message often hidden by the words.
He's a mirror who shows me my humanity
and tricks me into laughing when I'm feeling too severe.

He's a soft but steady one, a resolute but gentle one,
whose wisdom and irreverence work in harmony.
He's a melody of key changes, unopposing opposites,
teaching me the nuanced beauty of allowing things to be.

He's a problem-solver, a get-up-and-doer,
a grab-the-bull-by-the-horns creator of his reality.
He's a maker of things, a builder of dreams,

a manifester, intention setter, a second-natured visionary.

He's a cowboy and a rebel,
a musician and a fisherman,
a rock-stacking, river-rafting
captain of adventure.

He was my advocate when I couldn't be,
he met my harsh with loyalty,
and when I was lost,
he always made me feel seen.

My dear sweet dad, I owe so much of who I am
To the ways that you are you.
You will always have a home with me
In my endless gratitude.

Chapter 14
Day Six

My cousin Dylan, his partner Tatiana, and I were outside in the late afternoon glow. Dylan was stacking rocks in the garden, an exercise that had become a meditation for us, centering us through the delirium, and Tatiana and I were lying on a quilt in the grass. My bones felt weak and creaky, my muscles tight, my shoulders tense. I'd been chest breathing and clenching my jaw for weeks, and my heart had been palpitating. There was a vacuum in my solar plexus that made me feel like I was always just about to go over the highest peak of a roller coaster, and I know I'm not alone in this experience of anxiety.

Monika, our family medicine woman, intuitively got us onboard for a group yoga session. The three of us grabbed blankets and mats, and Aunt Nancy joined in. We were led through soft stretches that deepened our breathing and guided us back into our bodies. We bowed, we surrendered, we prayed. They say where two or more are gathered, the prayers are intensified, and I can guarantee that we were all praying more genuinely than maybe ever before. My prayers didn't have words, but they carried my humble wish for peace, inner and outer, for all of us. I could not extend my prayers to all sentient beings, as I normally do, because the scope of my compassion, just like my vision and my awareness, was limited to right there, right then. I recognized that I'd lost all concept of what was happening in the rest of the world.

We finished the class with a soft relief in our eyes and moved into meditation in Savasana, also known as "corpse pose." We'd just been given the most precious gift imaginable to us right then——a break. A moment of true, nurturing self-care. I glanced over at Dylan, who was more like a brother to me than a cousin while we were growing up, and felt deeply for him. He's reserved and tends to keep his thoughts and feelings to himself, but even so, I knew this was hitting him hard. He and my dad had a close relationship, maybe even closer than the relationship I currently shared with my dad. Who knows?

I noticed the insecurities this thought was showing me. The truth is that I'd been out of the country for nine years, and prior to leaving, I wasn't very present anyways. But my cousin had been there this whole time. He'd spent birthdays, Father's Days, Seahawks games, and family gatherings with Dad, whereas I'd shown up for an occasional phone call and a summer visit that went by so fast that by the time I was over the jet lag, it was time to leave again. I felt the weight of that guilt.

As we slowly rose up from Savasana, we gave Monika our gratitude for working her healing magic on us once again—her massages had already been getting many of us through. She was my cousin too, but where Dylan and I were just one year apart and had grown up together in Washington State, she was twenty years older than me and lived in Michigan with Dad's side of the family. Sometimes she was a guardian whom I looked up to, and sometimes she was a friend I drank margaritas with and talked about boys with. Our relationship had taken different shapes over the years, despite my inconsistent and sometimes nonexistent connection with the Michigan family, but she and I had always shared a special bond.

When I was fifteen and just getting through the most rebellious of my difficult teenage years, my parents sent me to Michigan for the summer under the pretense that I would be helping Monika with her toddler and five-year-old while she took care of her newborn son. At the time, I was more familiar with her in photographs than in person, but my dad and she were tight. I later pieced together that, although she was in need of an in-house nanny and my help was very appreciated, the main motivation for shipping me across the country to spend the summer with people I barely knew was to give my parents a break, keep me out of trouble, and give them the space to figure out if there was a separation in their future.

I had been struggling with substances, isolation, anxiety, depression, self-harm, and an eating disorder since twelve years old, and she gave me the space to be myself through whatever I was going through without making a huge deal out of it. I remember feeling held but not coddled or suffocated. I felt seen without being called out. Over the years, a mutual respect and admiration developed between us, although she still always takes care of me when she can.

I think she had taken on the task of making sure I got through my dad's process with enough support. Mom was deep in it, didn't have a lot of space for what I may be going through, and no one would have expected any different from her. Everyone else was also spread so thin, emotionally and logistically, but Monika came with me to take the dog down the street to the park, sneaked behind the garage to share an occasional cigarette with me, and talked with me about what mattered to me right then—the subtle world of energies and all things esoteric and healing, which she happened to be extremely passionate about.

My second day there, I'd told her about the hypnotherapy regression with Michelle. Instead of reflecting the skepticism and disbelief of most people who heard the story, her face had lit up. Her smile said, "You've discovered the Great Mystery." It's nice having someone to talk to who believes there's more beyond death than Heaven and Hell or complete nothingness—the two options many of us are given to build our geocosmovisions around.

My parents would probably have identified as agnostic, although I'd heard them dedicate little conversation to the questions of who we are, where we come from, why we're here, and where we're going. I was raised without any spiritual practices other than some Zen meditation when

I was a teenager, and I'd always felt like that was missing for me. I'd asked my mom when I was a kid to take me to church, and she'd agreed, despite having left the Lutheran Church after her parents passed when she was still young. What I'd found there hadn't given me any satisfying answers.

My dad's side of the family, those who hadn't strayed from their religious path, were Dutch Reform, and two of his sisters had become evangelical in their spiritual beliefs. They were currently wrought with fear and anxiety because they believed, without an iota of doubt, that their sweet baby brother would be going to Hell in a matter of days. He had run away from the Christian cult, in his own words, which he'd held a leadership role in during his late teens, abandoning religion entirely. Unless he invited Jesus Christ back into his heart, he'd be dragged down into the underworld, and they desperately wanted to save him. Believing what they believe, I can't blame them.

Monika was the only person in the house whom I could truly be myself with—unfiltered, uncensored, and unselfconscious. We could talk about life after death, life before death, death that lingers around the living, and all things in between. Sometimes it felt like she had the answers I was looking for, and other times it felt like she'd wandered so far out into the astral that she'd gotten lost. I had no idea what was real anymore. Her nonchalance when talking about spiritual shields and archangels was both refreshing and confusing, but, at the end of the day, I would have felt utterly alone in all of this without her there.

Chapter 15
Day Seven

WE WERE ON PAUSE. THE house was still, so still that it felt like we were suspended in time. The director had cut the recording, and we, the actors, were between takes, just waiting to start shooting the next scene.

Dad's family had decided to go back to Michigan. They were vacillating between continuing on to Alaska or heading straight back home. Nobody knew that this was going to happen, not even my dad, but, miraculously and conveniently, his siblings and Monika had planned a vacation to Alaska together for these exact days and therefore already had the time off to come be with us. All they'd had to do was reroute their trip and come to Seattle.

They'd left the day before and it was just us again, the immediate close family, the last ones hanging on. Dad required very little attention at this point, and it felt like we were now able to let out that big sigh we'd been holding in. The production no longer required so much crew and technical staff, and we could let our guard down a little bit, stop performing and curating, and just be.

I'd just woken up from a nap, one of those unavoidable ones that somehow leaves you at least equally as sleepy and disoriented as before you fell asleep. I heard voices in Dad's room, and some commotion. I pushed myself up and out of bed, extending my arms to the ceiling. A big yawn brought me partially back to reality, whatever that was. The commotion continued, and I thought I heard laughter. *Laughter?* That's medicine I hadn't had in a while. I opened the door and crossed the hall.

Mom, Tatiana, and Dylan instantly froze as if they'd been caught doing something wrong, which, some would argue, they had.

"What in the world…" I was smiling through my bewilderment, having walked in on the three of them looking like they were getting dressed for Carnaval or Mardi Gras. There was my dad, motionless in his bed, while the three of them played dress up with old Halloween costumes and ridiculous articles of clothing that had been dug out of my parents' closets.

I couldn't help but love the three of them even more for their insanity and irreverence. How inappropriate to play games like that while Dad was ending his life, much less in his room with him, and yet, I felt the urge to join them. I reached into the closet and pulled out some elf ears on a headband. I glanced at my cousin, who was wearing my mom's long purple felted jacket and leaning on my dad's hooked cane, with a flatcap on his head. I couldn't handle it. Tatiana was wearing a monkey costume, and my mom had on a witch's hat.

"We are bequeathing," my mom said, as if that was going to make any sense to me. "I've bequeathed Dylan with my furry cloak and your dad's flatcap."

"Everyone leaves and our true colors come out," I said, trying to stifle the laughter bursting out of me.

"Yeah, our true colors of crazy," Tatiana said.

Dylan and I doubled over trying to contain ourselves, tears rolling down our cheeks. I was reminded of the laughing fits that would take over us as kids—we were powerless to those fits.

My dad would appreciate this, I knew he would. He would appreciate that we'd been in this for seven entire days and had finally lost our marbles. The sane, put-together people had left and now it was just us, the weirdos who had no idea where the line was between normal and crazy. The immature ones, the goofy ones, the ones with no sense of respect—or maybe the trauma we were living with was so great that our psyches had reached their threshold and the only way to survive was to make light of it all. Maybe this laughter was the only medicine that could get us through.

Chapter 16
Day Nine

Day Nine came to end, and my sense of what was real and what was an illusion had never been less reliable. They kept telling us, "I think today is going to be the day," and so we'd get all worked up, say our goodbyes for the millionth time, and then nothing happened. We held our breath in a continuous state of tension and alertness but were waiting for nothing. Because nothing was happening.

The other day something had happened, but not the thing we were waiting for. It must have been on Day Six, or maybe Seven—I didn't know what time was anymore. On that day, his breathing pattern changed. His soft and restful inhalations and exhalations turned into sharp gasps, two or three times per minute. At first I thought he had stopped breathing entirely, so I put my ear next to his mouth to listen, and when he gasped, I was so startled I jumped back. After hours—or days, I don't know—of the gasping, the rhythm had slowed down, only to lend itself to something even more unsettling. They call it the death rattle.

I don't know how to describe it. I think it's something that you've either heard or you haven't, and there's no way of transmitting the feeling that sound creates inside you to another human. When the rattle started deep in the caverns of his chest, I'd felt a cold and otherworldly presence and couldn't shake the image of the Grim Reaper with his scythe from my mind. I saw him everywhere, as long as I could hear the rattle. It was bone-chilling. I was terrified.

Then I felt guilty for being afraid. How could this man, my dad, who had become so kind and gentle over the course of his life, frighten me? I sat down in the plush, gray chair next to the bed and looked death right in the eyes. Had they gotten even bluer? They were glossy and far away, half-closed. They looked like glass. I sat with him and stared into those distant, ice-blue eyes until I wasn't afraid anymore. I refused to be afraid.

The same day the death rattle started, Monika asked me if I thought his soul had left his body. My first thought was no. I thought his soul was still in there, making peace with the life it had lived in this incarnation. I didn't know if he could hear us anymore though. I thought he was in a private room with himself, doing some deep evaluating, accepting, and letting go. For him, the material world was no longer relevant. He'd moved into another space, and our words, touch, music, essential oils, and cheek kisses had faded into the background. His work in Earth School, at least in this body, was almost done. He was no longer thinking with his mind but was feeling and experiencing with a different part of himself. He'd returned to his essence. He was no longer Dad, Bruce, brother, husband, uncle, friend. He was light. He was love. He was on his way home.

    I felt trite and foolish talking to him as if he were still Bruce Vredevoogd, my father. The things I would say, the books I would read, the stories I'd tell—they all seemed so trivial when compared to the profound work I believed he was doing then. I'd sat with him on different occasions over the last few days, but I hadn't felt connected to him. I sometimes put on some music, but I never talked. He wasn't ours anymore. He didn't need our sadness, wallowing, or grief. He needed quiet, and he needed love. Love, love, love.

Chapter 17
Day Ten

I HAD THREE NIGHTMARES LAST NIGHT, one after another. Is dream déjà vu a thing? In the middle of this nightmare, in which my mother drove off a cliff and into the ocean, I had the distinct feeling of having been there before. I supposed that was a decent representation of my current waking state. Horror and confusion.

In the dream, she emerged from beneath the water screaming and gasping for air. I dove in to help her. Shards of glass had pierced her flesh and were stuck inside her body. I began to pull them out, but I could barely see the scale of the damage because we were submerged in the water. As I wrenched a big shard from the back of her neck, I knew it would be the end for her, she was going to bleed out. The following two dreams were equally gruesome.

My body was resisting something, fighting a good night's sleep, fighting settling in. I didn't feel like myself. I was doing yoga daily. I'd taken a few walks. I was meditating. I was taking my supplements. But there was a tightness in my lower chakras that I could not release. It was a jitteriness, a nervousness. As Tony had said the day before, it was always calm in the eye of the storm, and I was afraid to get comfortable. This sleepy, dreamy, floating-through-clouds-between-worlds feeling seemed like it was going to last forever, but the storm was coming.

Chapter 18
Day Eleven

THE QUIET STILLNESS OF MY aunt's little red cabin tucked in the evergreen trees was both comforting and unnerving. I'd stayed there the last two nights to get some space, to look out a different window, to breathe air that wasn't laced with death. Since the Final Fast had turned into a lifestyle for us, I'd decided to teach a couple of online classes, just to give my days some structure and to do something that would help bring me back to earth. I wanted some privacy for that, so Lulu had offered to stay with my mom and let me stay there.

Whenever Agnes had to take some nights off, my mom, her sisters, and her friend Max organized a rotating schedule for the medication. Again, I was grateful that no one asked me to be part of the morphine administration team.

I sipped my coffee and connected to the online classroom to meet my student, just as I had the day before, but the connection kept breaking up. We both had full Wi-Fi signal, but after struggling for ten minutes to understand each other, we decided to reschedule. What was going on? My next class was an hour and a half later, so I decided to go back to my parents' house. It felt wrong to stay there by myself.

I walked into the house to find it unusually still. Aunt Nancy was reading a book on Dad's mechanical chair. She was brightened by the morning sunlight coming in through the window, and she seemed at ease. I saw Lulu outside, gardening. Nancy told me that my mom had gone to the pharmacy to refill the morphine script again.

"I think you should go sit with your dad a bit," Nancy said softly. "He might be close."

This again. I felt myself contract. They'd said he was close on Day Four. Tiffany had advised me not to go get a coffee from the drive-thru down the street on Day Six because she didn't want me to miss it. And here we were on Day Eleven doing the same old dance. I didn't want to sit with him. It wouldn't make any difference to him whether I was there or not. My gut clenched, but I went to the room anyway. Max was reading the newspaper on the armchair. She gave me a kind smile before standing up to give me her seat.

It was even more still in this room than in the rest of the house, and yet there was something fragile about this quietude. It was brittle, like a thin sheet of ice. I had to move carefully so as not to break it. He hadn't moved a muscle in days, not even to blink, even though his eyes were gently open. I'd only just sat down, but something felt different. He started taking soft, little sips of air. I felt the unmistakable urge to play the whale song and didn't know why. Max went to get Nancy and Lulu.

When the first note of the song sounded, his eyes opened up all the way. I gasped. This was not a muscle spasm. He was reacting to the music. His left eye closed, then his whole face started to move. His mouth opened wide, and his thin, almost translucent skin was stretched tightly across his cheekbones. *Is he in pain? It's scary, but I can't look away,* I thought. The slide guitar sang the whale's call—it was calling him in. Lulu whispered that he was smiling, but I knew otherwise. He was leaving his body, his soul separating from its vessel. A minute went by. His expression relaxed.

The death rattle was back—he had one foot out the door. I held my breath as the song ended. It was almost over. The rattle was gone. His breathing had softened. The last note. He took a breath.

Then, we waited for another breath.
There wasn't another breath.
Still no breath.
No breath.
No breath.

Time of Death: July 12, 2021 at 10:26 a.m.

Chapter 19
The End of the Fast

THE SILENCE WAS SACRED. THIS stillness was unlike any other. He had been motionless for what felt like ages, but now he was like a sculpture. I watched as Max reached over and gently closed his eyes. My aunts both held me in an embrace. I felt the wetness of tears on my shoulder without knowing which of us they belonged to. Probably all three.

This was the moment that everything had been building up to. The culmination of the past eleven days, the past four months, the past seven years. He did it. He made it to the other side, and on his own terms.

The others quietly filed out of the room and left me to grieve. I looked at him and realized that I'd never seen a dead body before. His skin was already losing color, and I could feel in my bones that this body was just a composition of minerals and organic matter and that he was already somewhere far away. But I didn't doubt for a moment that he was *somewhere*.

I reflected on the journey he'd completed, and on the journey he was just embarking on. It's heartbreaking how proud of him I was. It cracked me open, and I began to sob. I fell to the ground. I'd never lost anyone before. I was fully immersed in the unknown.

In the midst of my collapse, I thought of my mom. She'd be home any minute, and someone would have to tell her. *It should be me.* I got up and wiped my eyes just as a car pulled into the driveway. It was Tiffany, the hospice nurse. I raced outside, not wanting her there when my mom got there—her energy was not something we had space for right then. I told her my dad had passed, and she wanted to come in and check his vitals to confirm. I asked her to come back later. She insisted. My mom would be there any minute—she needed to leave. She offered to stay to help support my mom, just not getting the picture. I asked her again to come back later. Then Mom was pulling up. Max came over and told her to leave, that this was a private and personal moment for the family that she wasn't part of, and I was filled with relief and gratitude. I didn't have the strength to be so assertive.

Tiffany pulled out of the driveway as my mom got out of the car. I waited for her on the front lawn, and as she walked toward me, she understood my expression. I gave her a hug.

"It happened," I said through quiet tears. I could feel her muscles fall limp. We stayed like that for a while. It was just me and her. Our journey began then.

Chapter 20
Beginning to Grieve

I READ SOMEWHERE ABOUT AN INDIGENOUS community in Northern Australia that has a special tradition. When someone in the village dies, every household moves a piece of furniture. Not something small like a lamp or a picture, but a table or a couch. Something consequential. This way, when the bereaved wake up the next day, they see that everything is different, and not just for them but for the whole community. At my house, not only had the furniture been rearranged, but the entire landscape had been altered. Where there were trees, there was now a meadow. Where there was an ocean, there was now a desert. Nothing was the same.

My dad was gone. I wanted to have it printed on a T-shirt so that everyone knew. It was the only thought in my head, and I needed people to know that before they interacted with me. How could they ask me if I wanted a paper or plastic bag for my groceries, or if I wanted cream or sugar, as if the world wasn't upside-down? Didn't they know that everything had changed, that nothing was the same? *Don't they know?*

The thing about grief is that it longs to be seen. It yearns for recognition, but it hates being patronized. We don't know how to talk about grief, nobody teaches us that in our culture. We know how to give hugs. We know how to bake cookies and send flowers. We know how to tilt our eyebrows up and say, "I'm so sorry for your loss." But we don't know how to hold space for grieving. We don't know how to be with a person and their grief without trying to fix it or make it more comfortable. We don't know how to be with grief because we don't know how to talk about death.

In some cultures, the bereaved wail and cry alongside the body, leaving no heavy emotion unexpressed. Cultures that haven't removed themselves so far from nature are still in touch with the rhythms and ancestral wisdom of the earth. They understand that death is the end of a cycle, but it isn't The End. They know that everything is cyclical. Where I'm from, we either disregard death entirely until we are forced to acknowledge it, or we spend our lives barely living, in fear of tempting it.

Chapter 21
November 2021

I HAD THREE DREAMS ABOUT DAD in the months after he passed. The first two were flashbacks to the eleven days of VSED. They felt like little trauma leftovers, like those dreams that mean nothing but just serve as a reminder of something that left a mark. The third dream was big and potent, one of those vivid dreams that leaves you questioning who actually puts the thoughts into your head, whether dreams are even of your own creation.

I had the big dream on his birthday, November ninth. I saw his fingers dancing nimbly across the ivory keys of a grand piano, from which classical music echoed and reverberated all around me.

"But you don't play the piano, Dad. You only tune them," I thought.

"Yeah, but here, where I am now," he answered, *"there are no limitations to my musical expression."*

When I woke up and opened my eyes, I could still hear the classical piano echoing throughout the room.

Chapter 22

I DON'T KNOW WHERE MY DAD is. I know his ashes are in the ocean off the Pacific coast of Mexico, on a beautiful island in Ottawa, in a lake between mountains in Washington State, at Mt. Shasta, and other magnificent places where he was taken and left.

My mom filled up little cloth bags and gave them to the guests at his wake, giving each of them the opportunity to bid my dad their own intimate farewell. I had been horrified when she told me about her plan to hand out little bags of my dad like party favors, but people seemed to appreciate it when it happened. Having returned to Spain just a week after his passing, I watched them on my laptop, outside on the patio under the starlight, where I live streamed the wake from across the world. I felt like an omnipresence, seeing all but engaging in nothing.

Katie stood up in front of everyone and read the eulogy poem on my behalf, and others took turns telling stories about my dad and speaking to his presence in their lives. I watched as they hugged and cried and then drank wine and danced with their shoes off, just as he would have wanted. I was his only child, and I wasn't there to share my words, to give hugs, or to help celebrate his life. Instead, I was alone, under the stars, my face lit up by the light of my laptop, watching it all through a screen.

It was a strange thing to grieve, or attempt to do so, when the closest person who had also had a relationship with the deceased was thousands of miles away. Sometimes it felt like I had made it all up, as if it were just a long, hazy, uncomfortable hallucination. I had gone from that untethered dream-state where I was floating in space as he died, straight back to my house in Málaga, a part of my life that had never been touched by my father. The sudden distance and jarringly abrupt change of scenery made the grief easy to detach from. My day-to-day life didn't remind me to grieve, and I wasn't going to remind myself.

Despite feeling far removed from everything we had undergone as a family and that I had undergone as an individual, something inside of me had been fundamentally altered in ways I was incapable of recognizing. One can't go through an experience like that and come out unchanged. Things that I had thought were important became mundane, boring even, and things that I hadn't understood before were suddenly sharp and clear. I had less patience for trivialities, and a greater sense of what actually mattered. The experience of being with my dad as he died was profound to the degree that life couldn't return to how it was before—the paradigm shift had been cataclysmic. I had been pulled in too deep to make it back up to the surface. The tectonic shift of his passing was so seismic that the earthquakes reached parts of my life that I never would have expected. Through the rumbling, I questioned everything—my relationship, my career, my place of residence, my sexuality, my life's purpose. No stone was left unturned, and no facet of my life was too sacred for scrutiny.

A cascade of monumental life changes ensued, including the calamitous ending of the relationship I was in and the two months of hell and psychological abuse that followed before I was able to move out of the house we lived in together. And shortly thereafter came the radical and unanticipated decision to leave Spain.

First, it was Mexico. Then, I considered Southern California. Costa Rica was a later candidate. Spain didn't make sense anymore because, just as that community in Australia had known, I needed things to *look* different. I needed the physical world to reflect that everything had changed, that nothing was the same. After a period of seesawing, it became clear that the only option was to go back home to Washington, to my mom, to my dear Pacific Ocean, to the earth and the air that had raised me. I needed to reconnect, return, reexamine, and rebuild.

My dad died on July 12 in 2021, and I moved back to Bellingham exactly five months later. It took three months for me to wrap my mind around leaving Spain, the place I thought I was going to spend the rest of my life, and two months for me to pack up and get home, but after spending nine years of my life there, that was basically the blink of an eye.

Chapter 23
December 2021

I moved from Spain into my mom's house, right into the room my dad had died in. My mom had nestled into the room where I used to sleep, so it was either this one or the tiny guest room. This room had a bathroom and hardwood floors, so I decided that with enough sage and palo santo, I could make it work. I cleaned it, cleansed it, and filled it with all of my tchotchkes, books, and shamanic tools. It frightened me how little I was affected by what these walls had witnessed. The room felt empty and void of any energetic remnants of last summer's nightmare—a projection of my own emptiness and a blaring marker of my dissociation.

I spent the winter deep inside myself, licking my wounds and maintaining a limited social life. My afternoons were spent in the forest with my dog, and my evenings were dedicated to my shamanic studies and spiritual practices. I cried on occasion, but I didn't cry for my dad, rather for the Mediterranean. My grief was derived from a longing for the life that I had so easily plucked myself out of and the fear that the one I had dropped myself into wouldn't compare. I woke up in the mornings after dreaming of the beaches and the hours of sunlight on the coast of Southern Spain. I didn't dream even once about my dad.

When people asked me why I had moved back, I told them that it was because my dad had died and I wanted to spend time reconnecting with my mom. It was true. Their faces would get soft, and their eyes would fill with the expected compassion. "Oh, it's really okay. I've made my peace with it," I would say. There was no need for anyone to feel uncomfortable, since I had clearly had a very mild case of grief, one which had worked itself out seemingly on its own.

Mom and I grew closer and started letting each other into our respective worlds. I shared my spiritual practices with her, and she became, herself, enthralled by the mysterious worlds of indigenous healing. We had great conversations around the fire about romance, addiction, childhood, the Great Mystery, and relationships. When

I started seeing signs and receiving messages that seemed to guide me toward seeking out a spiritual experience with mushrooms, I shared this with her. When the signs became so clear that I felt compelled to heed them, I asked her if she would be willing to accompany me on my journey and act as my "grounder." She agreed, faithfully and eagerly.

Chapter 24
April 2022

I SET MY INTENTIONS CEREMONIOUSLY. We built a fire, made an altar, and I drummed in the four directions to open sacred space for the ritual. We had come to Aunt Lulu's cabin. She was spending the winter at her home in Arizona, and it seemed like the perfect place to connect with the evergreen trees, listen to the birds, and have the space to commune with nature without the distraction of cars and neighbors.

Mom lovingly and carefully prepared the tea with the mushrooms a friend of mine had selected for this journey, and I sipped it, watching the flames flicker and fall. I tried to surrender, but what transpired over the next five hours was not the journey I had prepared for. I guess you can never truly prepare.

I didn't dance around with fairies and talk to the trees as I had hoped. No. Instead, I felt the most disconnected, separate, alone and forlorn that I've ever felt in my entire life. Weren't mushrooms supposed to do the opposite? I felt uncomfortable and cut-off and so incomprehensibly tired. The space–time continuum had shifted. Space was thicker, I moved through it slowly, and time became nonlinear. Language lost its sense, and I didn't like the feeling of talking. I was too far inward to do any outward expression.

I sat under a tree because I could barely withstand the weight of my body or of my sadness. Tears trickled down my cheeks, and my broken little heart just wanted to melt into the ground, give in to the pain and let its heaviness pull me into the earth. I told my mom I needed to go back to the house, curl up, and go into the sadness so that I could come out on the other side.

We arrived at the house quickly since we were only a few minutes down the trail through the trees behind my aunt's house, and I experienced a momentary sense of relief when I realized we were already back. I had thought we were much farther away. I turned on the heat and got as close to the stove as possible—a winter frost had crept up over me from within and had me trembling.

Nothing was right, and there was no way for me to feel comfortable. I moved to the couch, which felt hard and cold, and curled up under a blanket, which provided no warmth. I felt utterly stranded in that frequency of sadness. Everything else seemed futile, meaningless, and self-indulgent, and the only thing that had any integrity was heartbreak. Tears poured down my face in rivers.

Eventually Mom came in, and I was able to talk a little. I asked her how long it had been since I drank the tea and if it was going to stay like this. I asked her if I had been sad forever.

She sat down on the armchair next to the fireplace and had me sit on the floor in front of her so she could rub my shoulders.

Then it hit me. "I miss Dad."

As the words came out of my mouth, the real sobbing began—the snotting, drooling, head between my knees, gasping for breath, sobbing. She hugged me from behind, her eyes moist with tears. We stayed like that for a while.

"You're out there healing everyone else, but who's healing you?" she said in my ear.

That's when I realized I had been having a trauma response all of those months. All of the times that I'd felt creepy or guilty or just numbed out because of how little I seemed to care that my dad was gone had an explanation that didn't involve me being a sociopath. I was actually really, *really* sad.

"Of course you're sad, baby," she said. "We're all sad. I'm sad." She told me about doubts and regrets she sometimes had, wondering if she had done the right thing in supporting him. She also told me about something that had happened on Day Three of his fast.

He'd had a specific idea about what was going to happen over the course of the following days when he began his VSED journey. Things, however, went very differently than he had expected. There were issues with the catheter that made everything exponentially more complicated, the sudden lack of Parkinson's medication in his system had had instant repercussions, the morphine dose wasn't keeping him as comfortable as he had wanted, and he couldn't communicate with his friends and family, so he'd told my mom that things weren't going right and he wanted to try again in a little bit.

"I told him there wouldn't be a next time," she said. "It was now or never, because it was too hard on all of us to go through this with him again." Sometimes she felt guilty, but what other option did she have but to support him? And then remind him that this was what he had wanted, and if he stopped now, he wouldn't have the same level of support two weeks later when he decided to give dying another go?

She also told me that she had been so wrapped up in caretaking and facilitating that she barely connected with him over those eleven days. He would only call her when he needed to pee. It turned out I wasn't the only one who'd felt slighted. He did no bestowing, made no speeches, nor gave any loving last words to either of us. But what could we have expected from him? His mind had been on other, graver things entirely.

We cried together for really the first time. I was able to see that I was not alone, that we were all fucked up, that we all bore emotional scars and other consequences from what we'd been through last summer, and that we were all just in there, suffering, processing and reckoning on our own, in our own weird and lonely ways.

I had gone from floating in space while he died, straight back to Spain, where nothing about his death seemed real. Then, months later, I came back from Spain, where I was so far removed, and started living in the room where I'd watched him die. Dissociating was the only logical response.

"What we went through was traumatic," Mom said after I told her about this. "And what you went through in Spain was also traumatizing, and you were all alone. You're having a trauma response, babe. You're not a sociopath. You're not crazy, and you're not dead inside. You're experiencing PTSD."

I'd never felt more validated in my entire life. Of course I felt weird and crazy and detached and numb and confused and disconnected and desperate and tired and anxious and hollow and ridiculous and empty, and every other emotion that dances around but never fully surrenders to sadness. My subconscious had been protecting me from going all into the sadness too hard and too fast, but it was time now. The forest hadn't held me like I had wanted her to because she knew I needed to make it there, deep into the dark place, in order to feel human again, in order to reconnect with my own healing journey.

I needed to be soft with myself, treat myself gently, and not give so much away to the outside. I'd broken out of my cocoon too fast, and maybe I needed to crawl back in for a little while. That's what the mushrooms wanted to show me. That was their medicine. I needed to grieve.

Chapter 25
July 12, 2022

I DIDN'T KNOW WHAT TO EXPECT as the one-year anniversary of my dad's transition of form approached, which is how I had learned to call and truly regard his passing. The day his fast had begun a year prior, I called my mom on the phone from the island of Kaua'i, where I had recently moved. She said she had been starting to feel a little anxious, as the weather was getting hotter and the time of year had been reminding her of what we were doing at this time last year. We both wondered how we were going to feel as the days went by and what reaching that eleventh day was going to be like.

"I don't think it's going to be a huge deal," she said, maybe believing it, maybe trying to convince the both of us. "The worst part was the buildup, anyways."

"Yeah, I think you're right. I mean, it's just a normal day. The grieving has been going on this whole time, and I've really processed a lot of that heartbreak, so I don't think anything catastrophic is going to happen for me emotionally."

I received emails and messages from Dad's family in Michigan and gave and received lots of love from my immediate family—and I know that even those I didn't communicate with were feeling and remembering. Mom and I checked in every couple of days, and it was clear that a sort of energy had set in; a cloudy, dreamy, suspended-in-time energy that had a distinctly eerie aftertaste, very reminiscent of the energy of the Fast. We got through those ten days without too much trouble though, and on the night of July eleventh, I thought I had made it through the threshold unscathed. My mom and I had both talked about little rituals we were going to do the next day to honor him, but we truly weren't too worked up about it.

But, grief is not linear, nor does it ever end. It changes form and intensity, but it doesn't disappear. Sometimes it's comforting, and other times it sneaks up on you like a lion and rips you to shreds. It is an enigma. On the morning of July twelfth, a day just like any other, I opened my eyes and immediately began to weep. There was no time for thoughts or reason, only feeling. The weeping turned to sobbing, and I surrendered to the unexpected wave of emotion, allowing myself to be saturated.

One thing I can say for certain is that grief changes a person. It asks us to reinvent ourselves, because a part of us dies along with the loss and is swept away with it. We're forced to shift into a new identity in order to reckon with the part of us that's been torn away. But after the constriction comes expansion, and therein lies the gift. Grief, as relentlessly painful as it can be, offers an opportunity to reconstruct ourselves, to integrate the heartbreak, and to broaden not only our threshold for pain but also our ability to recognize and experience beauty. They say that our capacity for joy is directly correlated to our willingness to feel pain. Let this be an opportunity for us to experience shades of joy that we couldn't have otherwise imagined. Each day that goes by I am shown how with every true tear of grief I shed I can laugh that much harder when I do.

Martín Prechtel, a teacher of Tz'utujil wisdom, says that for the Mayans grief and praise are so interlaced that they are actually one and the same. We grieve what we've lost when it's gone and, in doing so, we praise it for having existed in our lives. We praise what we've got while it's here, and simultaneously, we're grieving how precious it is, and that one day it will be gone from our lives. Grief is gratitude for life, he says. So if we, as a culture, struggle so much to grieve with our whole hearts, what does that mean about our ability to appreciate the fullness and beauty of what's here with us, now? To the degree that we're afraid to grieve, I believe we'll be afraid to live.

This journey has been the biggest teacher for me thus far in my life. Over the past year, I've seen loyalty capable of renewing one's faith in humanity. I watched my entire family come together to support each other—a family that rarely exchanges birthday wishes. Friends made sure we had home-cooked meals every day, and the house was filled with flowers for weeks. Even the toughest of us became tender and vulnerable, allowing for seemingly impossible connections to be forged. My father's disease offered us a window into the complexities and nuances of human emotion, which, although difficult, indeed added to the richness of my own emotional expression. Through this harrowing experience, we had all laid the groundwork for becoming softer, more compassionate, and better people, who will now be able to hold space for others in ways we wouldn't have before. Thanks to what we went through and how we showed up for my dad and for each other, my family now has access to a deeper emotional experience, a stronger willingness to explore pain with curiosity, a bigger appreciation for and desire to connect with each other, and a greater capacity for love.

May this be his legacy.

Epilogue
November 2022

I POURED A GLASS OF RED wine and took it, along with an American Spirit cigarette, as an offering. I lit some incense and laid down in the grass in the mango grove on the farm on Kaua'i where I'm living. As I watched the moon rise over the garden, the whale song danced in the trees. The leaves rustled, and I felt him. It was his birthday, the second one since he died.

The evening before starting his fast, he'd pulled me aside and asked me to tell his story. The request had seemed so clear at the time, albeit a huge responsibility, but now that I'd just finished writing the final chapter of the manuscript, I wondered.

"You asked me to write your story, Dad. But I don't think I did that," I said to the sky. "What did you want for this book? Did you want to empower people in your position with another option? Spread awareness about Parkinson's Disease? Tell the story of your journey and struggles? Inform people about VSED? This book is for you, Dad. What do you want it to be?"

I sat in the light of the full moon with my questions, and I heard an answer.

"Screw all that other stuff. I just want the story to tell how much I love you and your mom."

A tear trickled down my cheek.

I told my mom about the experience over the phone the next day. She let out a sigh, and I could feel her heart soften as she received his message.

"The man never breaks character, even in the afterlife," she said jokingly. "What do you want me to do with your body, Bruce? 'Do whatever you want.' What kind of funeral do you want Bruce? 'I don't care.' What do you want me to write in the book you asked me to write about you? 'Screw it, write whatever you want.'"

We laughed, and we appreciated. We visited memories of hilarious misadventures, like the time he capsized the MiniCat when they were sailing together, just after saying, "Let's see how fast this baby can go!" And another time when we were sailing with my elderly grandma and a fellow boater sailed over to exchange some harsh words because he thought my dad had messed with his fishing lines, to which my dad responded, red, "Don't speak like that in front of my mother, you foul-mouthed rascal!" Or when he was teaching me how to navigate a big raft down the San Juan River, and just after explaining how "it's all in the approach," his famous last words, we heard, "Oh, shit!" and were slammed into a rock and the whole crew had to come help us out.

There are certain things that he will always be remembered for. Root beer barrel candies. Flatcaps and sweater vests. Pickleball and Afro-Cuban jazz. John Deere tractors. Peppermint-flavored wooden toothpicks. Papa Murphy's pizza and the Seattle SuperSonics. Eggnog lattes spiked with dark rum. Handkerchiefs in his back pocket. But the most important thing for him to be remembered by is how deeply he loved. His friends, his family, his pets, his work. And just so it's clear, because he wanted it to be, he loved my mom and I to the moon and back.

If this book moved you, first, let me say that I am honored and humbled. Then, I extend an invitation for you to leave a review with your favorite retailer to help this reach other readers.

Author's Notes

As you've read, music has been an important part of my journey with my dad on this earth. Below is a list of the songs mentioned in this memoir, as well as other music that has been woven into our lives.

"Grant's Corner" – Jerry Douglas

"If I Had a Boat" – Lyle Lovett

"El Carretero" – Buena Vista Social Club

"Angel From Montgomery" – John Prine, Bonnie Raitt

"Pachamama" – Beautiful Chorus

"She Loves to Ride Horses" – Guy Clark

"Cosmic Dancer" – Valerie June

"Imagine" – John Lennon

"Tennessee Stud" – Johnny Cash

"Clay Pigeons" – John Prine

"Don't Know Why" – Norah Jones

"That's Where I Belong" – The Notting Hillbillies

Books that helped me heal.

Living Beautifully: with Uncertainty and Change
by Pema Chödrön

The Smell of Rain on Dust: Grief and Praise
by Martín Prechtel

On Grief and Grieving: Finding the Meaning of Grief Through the Five Stages of Loss
by Elisabeth Kübler-Ross M.D.
and David Kessler

Notes on Grief
by Chimamanda Ngozi Adichie

Way of the Peaceful Warrior: A Book That Changes Lives
by Dan Millman

Revolution of the Soul: Awaken to Love Through Raw Truth, Radical Healing, and Conscious Action
by Seane Corn

Many Lives, Many Masters: The True Story of a Prominent Psychiatrist, His Young Patient, and the Past-Life Therapy That Changed Both Their Lives
by Brian L. Weiss

About the Author

KATE VREDEVOOGD is a writer, healer, and teacher from Washington State who has made both Spain and the Hawaiian Islands her home at different periods of her life. She values connection, self-inquiry, and traditional healing frameworks. Through her writing she strives to open up thought and dialogue around the vastness, ambiguity, and spiritual-nature of the human experience and to invite readers to explore the depths and nuances of their own emotions.

Explore her healing work:
www.colibrialchemy.com

Read more of her writing:
www.wanderlustwords.com

Other Books by Kate Vredevoogd

From the Same Quiver: A Confessional Tale of Wanderlust, Friendship and the Pursuit of Self-Identity

Words of Wellbeing, A to Z

Palabras de Bienestar (Spanish Edition)

www.ingramcontent.com/pod-product-compliance
Lightning Source LLC
Chambersburg PA
CBHW060359080526
44583CB00012B/392